The **2020** HANDBOOK for Mitigating the Impact of Pediatric Protocol-Toxicity, ASDs and Autism on a County's Population

What Can a County

[City or Enterprise]

Do?

Dalva Evette Yarrington

Human Development and Information and Data Scientist
The ASD Equation Part II

What Can a County, City or Enterprise Do?

The **2020** HANDBOOK for Mitigating the Impact of Protocol Toxicity ASDs and Autism on a County's Population

ISBN: 978 -1070774015

Keywords: Regressive ASDs, Autistic Spectrum Disorders, Autism, Public Health, County Health Clinic, CETA, Jobs, Protocol, Green New Deal, Employment and Training, VISTA Alumni, Commission, CDC, NIH

What Can a County

[City or Enterprise]

Do?

Contents

What is a Handbook?

In this instance a Handbook is a concise, ready and current reference for mitigating the pervasive impact of ingested toxicity on public health, public safety and prosperity within a county, a city or a community.

Specifically, this handbook targets mitigation for the epidemic impact of Pediatric Protocol-Toxicity, ASDs and Autism on the County's Population.

The children impacted by adverse pediatric care protocol(s) have become adults and live with their rewired brains and in a society which has largely ignored their lack of opportunity and does not prepare public safety officers to accommodate their brain and processing differences. Something as simple as being slow to respond-- has been misconstrued as a "criminal" behavior. The injustice of failing to acknowledge and mitigate is on our watch.

What is Mitigation?

Mitigation is or can be efforts taken to reduce the harm, severity or duration of an adverse circumstance.

While humans are adaptable and can take adaptive measures individually at a pace that is remarkable, our governments and systems have tended not to be as agile as they could be.

Perhaps a pivotal factor is that an individual has to convince only one brain of the challenge being faced and governments often spend inordinate amounts of time in cya-denial and litigation. Meanwhile over the past quarter-century a systemic pediatric protocol error became an epidemic and that epidemic has become another and is still shabbily propped-up by denials.

This handbook is being handed-off to a needful community of leaders and followers.

This handbook is intended mitigation for the resulting lack of career and prosperity opportunities for the large numbers of persons born between 1991 and 2001 who were directly impacted by brain toxicity and subsequently diagnosed with mild to moderate ASDs or Autism.

If there are those who still can't phantom that a pediatric error can morph into a broad epidemic impacting a generation and a half of our children, here are a few facts to piece it all together.

A <u>Protocol</u> is an established and agreed-upon set of governing steps, practices, rules, terms and or conventions.

In health and wellness care a protocol may be referred to as a medical guideline or a method to be followed for optimal practice outcomes.

A <u>committee</u> is a group of people appointed for a particular function. A committee has duties which typically involve deliberation, investigation, analysis and reporting actions. A committee is a subordinate group by design.

When a committee is expanded or reconstituted a new mission statement and roles are typically necessary and are given. If a committee becomes subordinate to all or part of a new reconstituted group's authority, mission and duties operating procedures can become confused or even negligent.

When a committee of government appointed specialists become reconstituted into a committee involving other practitioners with other reporting and commercial allegiances the authority of the government appointed specialists can be compromised.

In the case of vaccine protocol such a shift occurred when the Centers for Disease Control panel was combined with the American Pediatric Association Vaccine committee members. The early 1990s saw shifts in the CDC committee, shifts in the number of vaccines given and the number given at a single dosing.

The timing of these changes in the protocol correlate with the emergence of higher rates of adverse pediatric outcomes, the ballooning of ASDs and learning disabled children.

There are questions which might have been asked and answered. "Just how many vaccines can be administered to an infant before the level of toxicity causes damage to brain cells?" Additionally, "Are some vaccine formula more toxic than others and which vaccines should not be administered at the same dosing?"

Other begging queries might be: Why were new vaccines introduced when they were and why is the work of said "government" committee no longer available to researchers?

<u>Toxicity</u> is poisoning from exposure to a substance or mixture of substances.

Brain toxicity is when a substance or mixture of substances impairs the brain's function. The level of brain dysfunction correlates with the level of substance exposure, frequency of exposure and brain age.

In the case of ASDs, brain cells are destroyed and the brain as an organ attempts to rewire itself as a repair.

A "brain specific" rewire then requires a patient specific care plan. When pediatricians are not being trained to recognize adverse vaccine reactions or postnatal toxicity many children went undiagnosed and when the suspicion of a systemic cause surfaced, it became even more difficult to get reliable information and a good diagnosis or care instructions.
The level of inventive treatments and care plans created by caregivers for this epidemic is a clear indication that pediatric health care practitioners failed a generation of children in regards to detecting an epidemic.

The push to prescribe psychotropic drugs to children for classroom management should have been a flashing red light-- instead it was simply a cash register ring for pharmaceutical companies.

In many of the cases of Autism or ASDs prior to the 1990s it was more likely that substance use during gestation was suspected.

However, that could never be tagged in the current epidemic numbers as an origin and the fact that more male children are impacted by ASDs than females present additional suggestions of a systemic origin.

Brain Age and Vaccine Contents

Brain age and the ability to withstand a stacked vaccine dosing have been found to be correlates. In a family with multiple children impacted brain age and outcomes were remarkably different.

There is evidence that soldiers who were given stacked vaccines in WWII in the Rocky Mountains experienced unusually high incidents of ARF (Acute Rheumatic Fever). Many doctors practicing in the 1990 were ill-equipped to recognize, diagnose or even acknowledge that ARF could be an adverse effect of vaccine dosing.

Some children with ARF were treated improperly and assaulted with even greater toxic episodes causing more dire health conditions along the Autism Spectrum.

Since the United States has been administering vaccine cocktails since the 1930s, there should have been significant awareness of the potential for toxicity and therefore adding additional vaccines to a regiment should have come under vigilant levels of review by government stakeholders and the targeted population.

That is just it, they the targeted population were infants and presumably would have no advocates armed with enough data to push back at the toxic overloading before the epidemic unfolded.

Children who were diagnosed and treated by detoxification, gastrointestinal monitoring and remediation or whose brains were more mature appear to have had better rehabilitative outcomes following protocol dosing errors. These individuals are in the mild to moderate range of ASDs.

Greater access to good care and early education were key factors in improving outcomes. Shorter stints on psychotropic prescriptions or receiving no psychotropic classroom management prescriptions also improved the mental health outcome of "mild and moderate" children.
These children became adults and are employable and in many instances great candidates for detailed research, catalog and database farming, archives and repetitive stock room tasking. Others are capable of far more.

A controlled set of encounters is best and working under the guidance of a mentor and review of a County Mental Health Advocate could reclaim their talents to the greater social and economic benefit of our communities.

Will you fix what you deny?

As long as dosing agencies deny that the toxicity which originated the brain cell damage and cell mutation came from a systemically administered protocol they will obfuscate from any comprehensive mitigation.

We can see the <u>outcomes of decades of denial</u>. Some untreated and underdiagnosed persons become school-shooters and we now have a horrid legacy of incarceration associated with this population.

The prison industrial complex seems to be the only segment of the economy that wants to monetize (use) these children. A county can see the data. A county is in a position to mitigate.

ASDs

According to the most recent posting in the National Library of Medicine's Medline Plus database, an <u>ASD</u> is a Learning Disorder or a Pervasive Developmental Disorder. Persons having ASDs may be characterized by impaired or delayed communication and socialization skills which are often most noticeable in unfamiliar environments or circumstances.

The NLM/NIH defines ASD as "a neurological and development disorder that begins in early childhood and lasts throughout a person's life."

In addition, many persons may have or have begun to manage varying levels of hyperactivity or attention deficits. The term "Spectrum" is used because of the broad range of symptoms manifested in this population of harmed individuals.

Autism

The definition for <u>Autism</u> has evolved and is still shifting in "authoritative" publications and databases. Some definitions are clearly obfuscation and others attempt to be as comprehensive as possible. There are also definitions designed to support a particular method or brand of treatment or product.

Some pharmaceutical companies have taken advantage of the denials and created a prescriptive "free-for-all" definition of Autism. But nothing that they promote is free.

There is often and in most diagnosed cases a hearing deficit and dead brain cells in that region of the brain is central to Autism as a disorder. Also accompanying Autism in these children and young adults has been lingering gastrointestinal difficulties. This is another indicator of the systemic substance origin of Regressive ASDs.

Regressive ASDs are maladies diagnosed after a healthy birth and infancy. These children were exposed to toxicity (substances) or toxicities subsequent to birth causing these maladies.

County Health Department

A <u>County Health Department</u> as discussed in this publication refers to the County entity charged to be on the frontline of community public health and reports to the county governing body.

County Health Departments administer vaccines and provide mental health services. Many of the children impacted by Regressive ASDs and a toxic vaccine "protocol" were given dosing by county health workers.

Many of these same County Health Departments have not implemented any comprehensive mitigating plan for the frontline of Autism.

A County

A County is an administrative subdivision of our elected government in the United States and within States with specific authorities, boundaries and political weight.

The United States has 3,142 Counties or in the case of Louisiana Parishes and over 100 other similar bodies not called counties or parishes but entities having similar authorities and political weight.

This group of over 3200 governing and empowered bodies can make a difference in the outcomes of persons impacted by Pediatric Protocol-Toxicity, ASDs and Autism.

What a County Could Do--

A county can take initiative.

A county can assess the numbers of persons born between 1991 and 2001 diagnosed on the Autism Spectrum and call for self-diagnosed persons and review claims for potential employment opportunities. This will require designating an existing HR staffer for the task or hiring a well-equipped designated staffer for this initiative. This assessment will give a working scope for the initiative.

If 100% of the persons screened qualify as mild or moderate on the Spectrum then the goal should be to secure a mentored introduction to employment for each person.

The length of each mentored opportunity may vary but the opportunistic intent should be as equal as is possible.

To avoid any confusion make sure that all notices indicate that the pilot or initiating phase of this employment initiative will focus on mild and moderate persons so as to not unduly mislead an eager person who requires a different level of accommodation.

The need to keep the initiative from being stalled is critical and persons with more severe disabilities should recognize and be told that this initiative is not a one-size-fits-all and is intended to break new ground with a specific scope and will be exempt from any undue scrutiny in terms of disability level bias. These concerns are bound to surface and because they are-- is not a good enough reason to do nothing.

After you have determined the size of the cohort you must focus in on what you can offer by assessing your workforce and requesting mentor volunteers and selecting certain others to participate. Voluntary participation is best and can be stipened in a number of ways, such as extra hours off, delayed work day or additional contributions to retirement.

Keep in mind that these citizens and voters have had little to no employment opportunities and would be thrilled to have a 12 or 16 hour opportunity once-a-week, once-a-month or even once-a-quarter. Thus 50 mentors could service two hundred mentees a month initially.

The justification for this initiative has been stated earlier in this handbook and the case should be easy to make to any county board or worker.

A critical component for success is properly matching mentors and mentees. This will require you to review a resume from the mentee which specifies their interest and learned skills to date. This data and the job descriptions of the county mentors should be mapped, matched and reviewed for best fits.

If a county worker is eager to take on several rotating mentees, verify with their supervisor and HR that there is a high potential for success for both the mentee and mentor. If ever there was an initiative that reveals flaws in your existing workplace this initiative will. That also means that the types of assessments and mentor mapping required in this initiative will be beneficial on multiple levels, likely improving County HR outcomes.

Before mentors and mentees are brought together to meet they must each in their group have an orientation to discuss and understand expectations. Success will depend greatly on what each is expecting at the outset.

It may be that some will opt out at the last minute, be prepared to thank them.

If the County decides that it will implement a program for one quarter each year then make sure that is what is done. The goal is success for all. Create a mitigation strategy that best suits your county's underemployed persons.

Clearly this program model is replicable. To target other groups take the same steps.

Here are a few questions the County will want to get answers to from the HR department before launching:

This data query was created for Dallas County Texas and is replicable for every county in the United States.

R & D Data

1. *Population total of Dallas County with date of numeration or estimate.*
2. *Population total of Dallas County with DOB between 1991 and 2001*
3. *Dallas County total Incarcerated with DOB between 1991 and 2001*
4. *Population of Dallas County with Disabilities and with DOB between 1991 and 2001*
5. *Any available data on categories of mild, moderate, severe disability or learning and physical disabilities.*
6. *Total number of paid positions on Dallas County payroll*
7. *Total number of existing volunteer positions in Dallas County workforce*
8. *Total number of internship paid and unpaid in Dallas County workforce*
9. *Total number of approved job shadows in Dallas County workforce in the past three years*
10. *Total number of apprenticable occupations in the Dallas County workforce*
11. *Total number of apprentices on the Dallas County workforce payroll*
12. *Total number of Dallas County employees over age 50, their job titles and job descriptions*

13. *Total number of Dallas County Employees under age 30, their job titles and job descriptions*
14. *Total number of new Dallas County positions anticipated in this calendar year*
15. *Total number of Dallas County positions being phased out in this calendar year*
16. *Forecasted Dallas County Job phase-outs*
17. *Total number of full-time positions held by persons over 50*
18. *Total number of part-time positions held by persons age 30 and under*
19. *Misc. Impediments, civil service etc.*

Please note that age 50 was targeted for workplace mentorship intentionally in lieu of reaching a level of mature patience and you may choose to approach selecting mentors differently.

As you can see a great deal can be learned from the initiating assessment.

To preserve stakeholder interest, report on outcomes and challenges at designated intervals. Launch, monitor and manage this initiative as if it is critically important, because it is.

We have all witnessed what it is like to have no response to the challenges hoisted on this population through no fault of their own and now we can be engaged and motivated by implementing a well-developed mitigation initiative.

The missing pieces are components your HR department already provides to employees. That onboarding should be tailored for the mentees. Use much the same orientation as you would give a temporary employee.

The main difference is the mentor and mentee relationship. While it might seem okay to just offer shadow or unpaid internships initially HR should determine when real work is occurring and compensation or actual hiring should occur.

If a mentee is hired any Mental Health support in place for the mentee should be carried over for as long as it is advisable.

Remember that only a very small number of these persons were left alone to become outcasts and "school-shooters."

Fixing this disparity is fixing our communities.

Deliverable Outcomes

- That 75% of the un-incarcerated persons on the Autism Spectrum with mild to moderate diagnosis and living in the County born between 1991 and 2001 will have had at least one workplace experience by the end of the first year.

- That the County workforce will have a greater understanding of the challenges, skills and attributes of this population.

- That the County workforce will have less fear and more empowered interactions with persons in this population segment.

- That income and skill levels for persons in this population segment have risen and further enriching the local economy.

- That mentors have benefited from participation on multiple levels.

- That this initiative has had a net positive effect on the County economically, socially and morally.

- That fewer of these persons are inadvertently or intentionally caught up in the prison industrial complex by ill-trained public safety workers and laxed parental or community supports.

Use the rest of this handbook for data collection, initiative roll-out and orientation.

Fill in your County data to begin.

The 2010 population of _____ County.

The current estimated population of _____ County.

Date of current estimate. _____

Source of Estimate_____

County population of persons born between 1991 and 2001. _____

County population of incarcerated persons born in the county between 1991 and 2001._____

County population of "all" incarcerated persons born between 1991 and 2001. _____

County population of persons born in the County with DOB between 1991 and 2001 and are enumerated as disabled._____

County population of "all" persons with DOB between 1991 and 2001 and are enumerated as disabled._____

Aggregate the population data on disabilities with whatever data you have on disability category (mild, moderate, physical disabilities, learning disabled etc.)

This data should identify the scope of the population you should seek to serve with this (mitigation, initiative, opportunity) program.

Sending queries to the known person will be your first attempt as verifying and establishing a set of primary stakeholders. A general public notice of opportunity about the initiative should be sent County wide or posted, prior to setting the primary stakeholder pool.

The query should ask about their interest in a County sponsored employment opportunity program which could provide a mentored workplace shadow experience or an internship and might lead to a part time or temporary paid job opportunity. Indicate that participation is voluntary. A willing participant gets the best results.

The second set of primary stakeholders will be the County workplace mentors.

From the County Human Resources Department and Payroll Department determine the total number of paid employees of the County _____. Be detailed and match the data to a specific employee. The Age of the employee, job description and age of the worker who holds the position are all important consideration in establishing a pool of workplace mentors for this program.

From the County Human Resources Department determine the total number of volunteer positions currently (_____) existing in County workforce and the total number of internships (_____) paid (_____) and unpaid (_____) currently existing in the County workforce. Identify the total number of current job shadow opportunities existing in the County workplace (_____). How many of these job shadows were approved by Human Resources? How many job shadow opportunities were provided by the County workforce in the past three years? (_____).

How many apprenticable positions currently exist in the County workforce? (_____). Hoe many apprentices currently work for the County (_____).

How many incarcerated persons work for the county (_____) in any capacity?

How many incarcerated person born between 1991 and 2001 currently or have worked for the county in the past three years? (_____)

What is the total number of County employees over age 50. (_____).

Of the total number of County employees over age 50, how many are willing to be trained to become a workplace mentor? (_____).

What are the job titles and job description of the County Employees who are willing to volunteer to become workplace mentors?

Match the job titles of the Mentor volunteers with the persons who voluntarily wish to participate in the employment opportunity initiative (the mitigation).

To further examine the nature of the County workforce determine the total number and percent of the county population who are under age 30. (_____)

Catalog the job titles and job descriptions of all County employees under age 30.

Catalog the total number of part-time positions in the County workforce including age of employee and job description.

Identify position with job description which are "too" complex or cumbersome, hard-to-fill and may be great opportunities for revision and perhaps a part-time spin-off position.

Review any forecasts of new County employment positions within the calendar year.

Determine if any of these forecasted positions could become part time and accommodations for program participants who are successful in job shadows or internships.

Identify any County positions scheduled to be phased-out over the next three years and seek to capture any knowledge-base from the impacted employees. Offer a mentorship opportunity if the employees will be transitioned to another job or are retiring. Position phase-outs can be an important tool in knowledge transfer and workplace orientation.

Subtract the total number of County positions held by persons over age 50 who have volunteered to be mentors from the total number of persons born between 1991 and 2001 seeking an employment opportunity and this will give you the scope of your initiative/mitigation.

Your primary stakeholders are the mentors and the mentees as well as the program coordinator and all citizens of the County.

Remember that onboarding and plenary are part and parcel to an experience. Diligently engaging these stakeholders will speak volumes about County leadership.

Allow for any workplace impediments, civil service or bargaining rules. The implementation of this mitigating initiative need not be disruptive. The initiative is designed to improve and enhance the wellbeing of the County and respond to a disparity in which the County is a stakeholder.

With justifications and feasibility in place there is only "will" left to implement.

This initiative can most successfully be handled by an experienced HR professional as a priority. If a separate program manager is put in place the individual or team should be well versed in workplace safety, accommodation and onboarding.

The costs associated with hiring and onboarding should incentivize the County to make the most of implementation and placements. The longer the placements the better.

If the county has a 6-9% disability rate in persons born between 1991 and 2001 then the goal should to be to create opportunities to match the challenge. Encouraging cities and other enterprises to establish similar goals is well within the scope of County leadership.

What Should We Expect of Cities and Enterprises?

Since this program model is highly replicable-- it may be adapted to any micro-niche entity (city, enterprise, township or congregation) incline to acknowledge and respond to the deficits and disparities imposed by the Autistic Spectrum Disorder Epidemic in the United States or globally.

At its core, this program model is a mentorship initiative and is morally crystalize-able by any standard.

We should expect it to be replicated and enhanced.

APPRENDIX

Public Title:

Vaccine Protocol, Practice and The ASD Equation

Abstract: *The longitudinal outcomes presented here occurred between May 1995 and December 2014 and focus specifically on the U. S. Autism "epidemic." These findings rest on research, archived data, observations, interventions and aggregated inquiry related to Cohort 80524.*
This report of findings is submitted by D. E. Yarrington, information [and data] scientist and health science library professional. The contents summarize information mapped in the ASD Equation and the ASD Equation including Regressive ASDs and gastrointestinal.

Findings

Etiology: Autism is avoidable. Regressive Autistic Spectrum Disorders are largely manmade protocol, care and practice errors.
Cohort 80524 revealed the sources of toxicity causing varying degrees of adverse reactions in each of the sample subjects. Stacked vaccine doses including preservatives containing mercury precipitated adverse reactions first manifesting months later as low-grade fevers and ARF. One of the subjects displayed severe chorea movements. Gastrointestinal difficulties emerged subsequently in two-thirds of Cohort 80524.

Toxicity: Subject one of Cohort 80524 was determined to have been stricken with toxicity causing fever and basil ganglia response (chorea) on May 3, 1995. The source of the toxicity was determined after case records and family history was collected and analyzed.

Sample subject one had exposure to vaccines only -- prior to hospitalization. After hospitalization sample subject one was exposed to multiple toxicities prescribed during a 58- day, error-laden inpatient episode.

Sample subjects two and three were exposed to additional over-the-counter fever remedies and pediatric acetaminophen.

All sample subjects received multiple vaccine doses from the same source in Zip Code 80524 within the course of two weeks in November 1994 under the prevailing protocol. Ethyl–mercury was present as a preservative in this protocol.

Multiple Toxicities: At some point multiple toxicities occur in the treatments of each sample subject. Multiple toxicities are unavoidable as a toddler develops and transitions seasonal and developmental markers such as teething and vaccine schedules.

The subsequent introduction of acetaminophen into the prescribed dosing of each sample subject may be a factor in so far as a spectrum of sensory dysfunctions and disorders emerge.

The off-standard use of steroids during what was to be a "hospital observation period" for sample subject one, presents further toxicity and other brain injury outcomes.

The possible implications for the gastrointestinal system from mercury poisoning were slower to emerge. However upon reviewing pre-hospitalization toxicity screens for sample subject one, clues may have been dismissed.

Gastrointestinal challenges emerged prior to identification of the clues in the toxicity screens and in fact caused a parental review of toxicity screens.

Multiple toxicity, brain damage and developmental regression from stroke and other medically negligent/unauthorized experimental health care given to subject sample one made the use of case records imperative in intervention and observation.

The holistic-like nature of the care given sample subject one from birth provided the baseline for a review of toxicity as etiology.

Adverse Effect Presentation Diagnostics: The presentation of fever occurred in all sample subjects. ARF occurred in sample subjects one and two.

The finding is that age may play a pivotal role in avoiding an adverse brain effect from [ ] ethyl-mercury poisoning.

The older the subject, the less brain dysfunction was observed, reported or diagnosed. Conversely the sample subject receiving the stacked vaccine dosing between [birth] age six months and 18 months experienced the most significant adverse effects/ manifestations. It is not known if the same age correlation can be applied to gastrointestinal damage.

It was found that pediatricians were ill-equipped to readily diagnose Sydenham's Chorea/ARF. Sample subject one was diagnosed by his research-scientist parent on May 3, 1995. This occurred three days after unauthorized further toxicity and harm was done by an infectious disease specialist using a monetized kitchen-sink diagnosis of encephalopathy. The differential diagnostic resources used by the parent were located in an adjacent hospital medical library.

Mercury and Ethyl-Mercury: Mercury can be toxic to humans. Ethyl-mercury was present as a preservative in vaccines given to sample subjects. The presence of mercury is not a new phenomenon.

The levels of mercury from vaccines impacting a pediatric brain changed over time with protocol. The capacity of the pediatric brain does not adjust to the increased levels of mercury in the protocol to protect itself.

Mercury toxicity can cause injury and mutations in the brain. Mercury was also present in the vaccine regiments given to late-teen inductees into the military in a stacked protocol.

Vaccine Protocol: The number of vaccines scheduled for infants and toddlers and the contents of vaccine formula has been and is subject to be changed. Vaccine Protocol Committees undergo personnel changes and protocol recommendations were changed between 1991 and 1994 and subsequent to a combined committee.

Cohort 80524

The Zip Code 80524 is located {Larimer County]
Colorado.   Colorado experienced a relatively large
number of teen and young adult incidents of suicide,
violence and other related challenges over the past
decade which can be associated with the 1991-2000
vaccine protocol timeline.

Interventions:
• 1995 Diagnostic Intervention
• 1995-2013 Data Collection and Data Archiving
• 1995-2010 Data analysis, Rehabilitative Care
intervention for sample subject one*
• 2010 Digital Data Conversions
• 2011 Data Review and Aggregation
• 2011 Documentary, Scripting and Production for "No
Precautions"
• 2012 -Provided Secretary of HHS and 15 other key
government and NGO decision-makers with
documentary demonstrating the complex set of
outcome which occurred when sample subject one
presented with an adverse reaction to vaccine protocol
in a pay-per-procedure facility utilizing HMO
practitioners. Documentary content was based on
sample subject one's health care and inpatient
outcomes.

Systemic Problems:

The availability of data for study related to vaccine
protocol development and vaccine committee changes
between 1991 and 1994 is problematic for investigative
purposes.

The granting of vaccine manufacturer immunities may
have preempted appropriate public health response.

Vaccine injury funding is inadequate and not widely
publicized.

The vaccine injury table is deficient. Additionally,
gastrointestinal injury was not included in the injury
table.

Efforts to protect a vaccine program without appropriate error management protocols has been a factor in the displacement of researchers and the shaming of practitioners and parents seeking answers and or review.

National/federal government administrative reviews need a different more navigable remedy infrastructure. A chief health officer (surgeon general) should be expected to publicly address any broadly impactful error and assure mitigation or remediation. Epidemics have typically received additional scrutiny and public health follow-up.

Physicians/pediatricians may have been permitted to broadly experiment on children presenting with adverse vaccine effects by simply calling the illness an encephalopathy.

Pediatric diagnostics should have in-flow clinical epidemiology. Facility risk managers have a completely different agenda than would a clinical epidemiologist. State medical review boards (peer boards) may have failed to police practitioners to the detriment of patients (children). Medical review board complaints which went unexamined or "whitewashed" should be reviewed as a big data initiative.

Impediments to remedy which filter access to legal remedy associated with ethnicity and income should be removed.

A generation of children, now young adults will need developmental learning support, life quality support and other mitigation causing an unanticipated burden on social security disability funds and household earners.

Prison industrialist/capitalist lobbied lawmakers for the role of keeper for these yet underdiagnosed children and young adults, who in most instances were unaware of the systemic etiology of their developmental, sensory dysfunction and behavioral troubles. In an effort to sort out these injured children testing was employed without the intent to offer humane and appropriate mitigating care and services.

Public Safety Officers have not been adequately trained to deal effectively (without mortally wounding) these sensory dysfunctional young adults.

Mental health services have in many instances worsened the problem by over-prescribing psychotropic toxins for ADD and ADHD. Additionally the presence of large quantities of these psychotropic toxins has increased the availability of substance abuse opportunities to siblings of sensory dysfunctioning, ADD and ADHD diagnosed children.

Congressional Responses:

The granting of vaccine manufacturer immunities may have preempted appropriate public health response. Appropriations for vaccine injury mitigation have been deficient.

Systemic Needs: Respond to the systemic problems listed above and more and improved FDA accountability for marketed drug substances is needed.

Cohort 80524 Information Dissemination:
        Documentary 2011
        10 Preliminary Papers 2013
        Study Registration 2014
        Findings Presentation
        Informal Discussions with Parent Groups and
        Colleagues
        Social Media Awareness Posts

Well-Documented Disparities: The unique nature of each brain rewire following toxicity and cell mutations can play a role in the under-diagnosis of Autism, Autistic Spectrum Disorders and related sensory dysfunctions. **Pre-existing ethnic health care disparities are playing a continuing role. Under-diagnosis and mitigation short-falls may be playing a role in teen and young adult suicide, violence and police involved shootings.**

Population Impact:

The most recent estimates of population impact suggest that male children are impacted more often than female children. Just since 2013 estimates of the prevalence of Autism have ranged from 1 in 88 children in the U. S. population to 1 in 36.

Further Study Warranted:

How likely is ethnicity to play a role in a diagnosis of Autism, Autistic Spectrum Disorders, Regressive ASDs or a pathway to public safety mishap or prison?

Interventions Needed:

- Autism and Regressive ASD Audit for all persons born between 1991 and 2000.
- Reparations for persons with evidence of Regressive ASDs who were documented as normal at birth and based on medical records developing into healthy toddlers prior to receiving the stacked vaccine doses containing ethyl-mercury.
- A formal apology to the parents and support for the caregivers who lost employment and retirement contributions due to systemic protocol error which the parents were obligated to subject their children to.
- A review and appropriate reprimand of practitioner pediatricians found to have knowingly experimented beyond Standard of Care and for profit causing addition toxicity and related inpatient harm.
- A reprimand of facilities knowingly underreporting practitioner errors and ARF.
- Data-mining all toxicity screens from Children's Hospitals and care facilities conducted between 1991 and 2000. Making the data available for further study.
- Publishing of all practitioner and facility review and reprimand findings.
- **Create a structured, monitored and well-funded life-quality (employment) opportunity program for all individuals impacted by this systemic error. REMEDY/response should be a part of the Public Health Act.**

Related Information Aggregation

1. Geier et al.: A two-phase study evaluating the relationship between Thimerosal-containing vaccine administration and the risk for an autism spectrum disorder diagnosis in the United States. Translational Neurodegeneration 2013 2:25.
2. Yarrington, D. E.: A Case for Case Records, The ASD Equation: Diagram. © 2013
3. Poses R M et al (1995) You Can Lead a Horse to Water — Improving Physicians' Knowledge or Probabilities May Not Affect Their Decisions. Medical Decision Making, the Official Journal of the Society for Medical Decision Making.
4. Geier DA, Geier MR: A meta-analysis epidemiological assessment of neurodevelopmental disorders following vaccines administered from 1994 through 2000 in the United States. Neuro Endocrinol Lett 2006, 27:401–413.
5. Institute of Medicine (2011) Adverse Effects of Vaccines: Evidence and Causality, Brief Report., p.1-6.
6. Yarrington, DE (2014) A Case for Case Records, The ASD Equation: Case Book. [Publication in Process] p.3-263.
7. Jonsen A R (1987) The Ethics of Pediatrics. Pediatrics, 18th Edition; Appleton & Lange: Pp. 1919, p. 9.
8. Pellerin D (1991) A new mode of Pediatric emergency care: the emergency and rapid diagnosis center... Bulletin de I Academic Nationale de Medicine; 175:3 p. 395-401.
9. Fenichol, G M (1988) Clinical pediatric neurology – a sign and symptom approach. WB Saunders Co; Philadelphia, p. 290-291.

Age (brain age) and dosing were pivotal actors in the destruction of brain cells via toxicity. **The resulting toxicity caused brain cell mutations and disrupted gastro-intestinal function as well as set the stage for other disorders, now referred to as ASDs**. Thus a protocol error is a variant actor in the origins of the toxicity involved in the Autism Epidemic.

A Case for Case Records

The ASD Equation:Diagram

A Defensible Explanation of Autistic Spectrum Disorder Etiology   © 2013 Dalva Evette Yarrington

Equation 1:

Stacked Immunizations 1994-2000 **=** No Adverse Effect **=** A nearly normal health care regiment with greater vaccine/fever vigilance and heart monitoring.

Equation 2:

A broadly utilized pediatric toxin or Stacked Immunizations 1994-2000 **=** Adverse Effect **=** Diagnosed (Ethyl-Mercury) Toxicity **=** Proper Treatment **=** Mild or Self-Limiting Impact. Nearly undetectable after a year (Brain-Basal Ganglia Self-Required). **=** Follow-up with monitoring for fever or ARF.

Equation 3:

A broadly utilized pediatric toxin or Stacked Immunizations 1994-2000 **=** Adverse Effect **=** Wrong Diagnosis **=** Improper Treatment (Error?) **=** Other maladies emerge along with Basal Ganglia mutations and possibly other brain toxicity. Brain may have been severely assaulted to a pre-birth level of functionality in some areas. Brain rewires to an unmapped level of functionality. **=** A full spectrum of disability and health care needs for a lifetime. Mental Health and self-management challenges (ADD, ADHD...) Learning Disabilities **=** A care-burden and life quality concerns. 1 in 88 Children with ASD 1 in 56 Male Children with ASD

Equation 4:

A broadly utilized pediatric toxin or Stacked Immunizations 1994-2000 **=** Adverse Effect **=** Experimental Diagnosis **=** Improper Treatment & High Potential for Greater Harm (Negligence?) **=** A lexical spectrum of outcomes most of which are treatment caused. Brain may have been severely assaulted to a pre-birth level of functionality in some areas. Brain rewires to an unmapped level of functionality. **=** A full spectrum of disability and health care needs for a lifetime. Mental Health and self-management challenges (ADD, ADHD...) Learning Disabilities **=** A care-burden and life quality concerns. 1 in 88 Children with ASD 1 in 56 Male Children with ASD

Version 1.1

© 2013 Dalva Evette Yarrington

A Case for Case Records

The ASD Equation: Diagram 1.2** Regressive ASDs including gastrointestinal

A Defensible Explanation of Autistic Spectrum Disorder Etiology

© 2013 Dalva Evette Yarrington

Counties are Here

Stacked Immunizations 1994-2000**	=	No Adverse Effect								

| A broadly utilized pediatric toxin or Stacked Immunizations 1994-2000** | = | Diagnosed (Ethyl-Mercury) Toxicity **After 3 cleanings of DPaT, a HepB and a Hib dose in the first six months of life, regressive disorders may well be underway according to Geier et al 2013. | = | Proper Treatment | = | Mild or Self-Limiting Impact / Nearly undetectable after a year (Brain-Basal Ganglia Self-Repaired) or **Regressive ASDs including Gastrointestinal | = | Follow-up with monitoring for fever or ARF or Mental Health and self-management challenges. (ADD, ADHD...) Learning Disabilities | = | A nearly normal health care regiment with greater vaccine/fever vigilance and heart monitoring. or A care-burden and life quality concerns. |

| A broadly utilized pediatric toxin or Stacked Immunizations 1994-2000** | = | Adverse Effect | = | Wrong Diagnosis | = | Improper Treatment (Error?) | = | Other maladies emerge along with Basal Ganglia mutations and possibly other brain toxicity. **Regressive ASDs / Brain may have been ... pre-birth level of functionality in some areas. Brain rewires to an unmapped level of functionality. | = | A full spectrum of disability and health care needs for a lifetime. Mental Health and self-management challenges. (ADD, ADHD...) Learning Disabilities | = | A care-burden and life quality concerns. 1 in 88 Children with ASD / 1 in 56 Male Children with ASD |

| A broadly utilized pediatric toxin or Stacked Immunizations 1994-2000** | = | Adverse Effect | = | Experimental Diagnosis | = | Improper Treatment & High Potential for Greater Harm (Negligence?) | = | A broad spectrum of outcomes most of which are treatment caused **Regressive ASDs including Gastrointestinal / Brain may have been severely assaulted to a pre-birth level of functionality in some areas. Brain rewires to an unmapped level of functionality. | = | A full spectrum of disability and health care needs for a lifetime. Mental Health and self-management challenges. (ADD, ADHD...) Learning Disabilities | = | A care-burden and life quality concerns. 1 in 88 Children with ASD / 1 in 56 Male Children with ASD |

Version 1.2**/3.10.2014

© 2013 Dalva Evette Yarrington

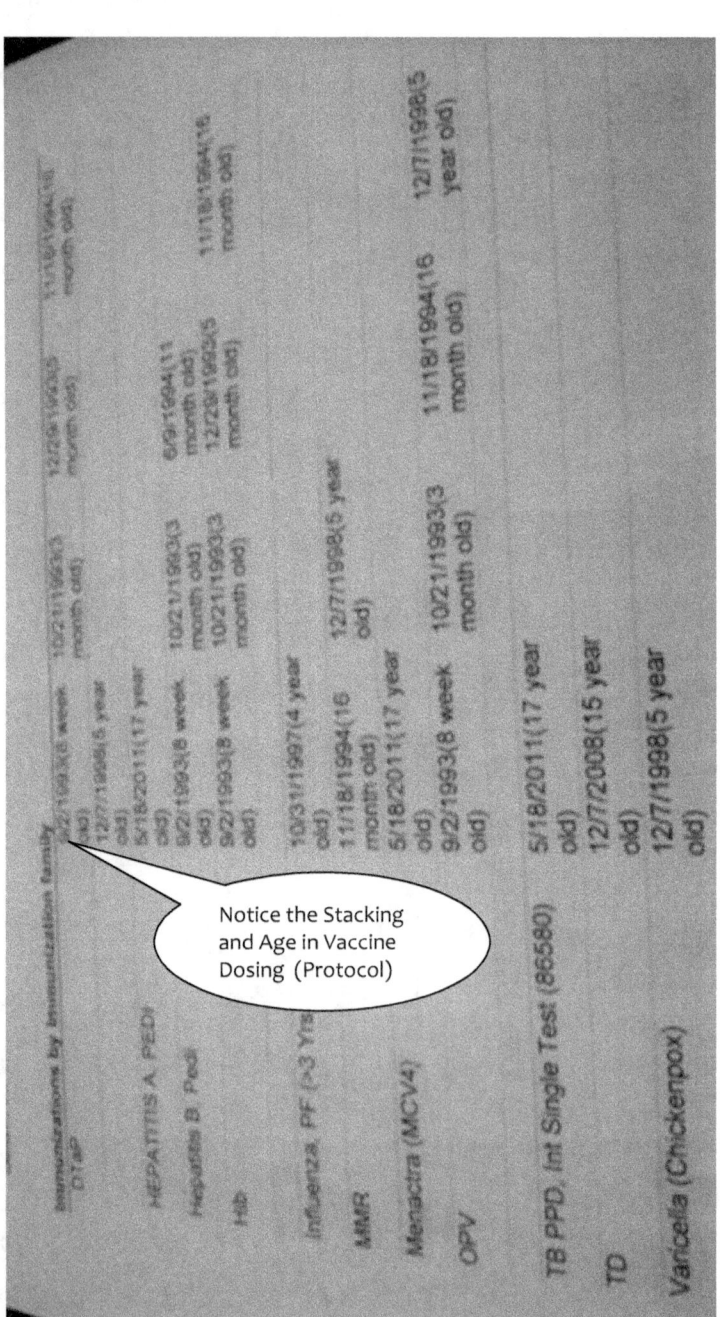

A County Shot Record

In Conclusion

Scientific Title: *Vaccines, Toxins, Sensory Dysfunction and Regressive ASDs in the U. S.*

The Autism Summary | Public Health Info-graphic | Brain Cell Mutations

Autism	=	Fetal or Infant Brain	+	Toxins	Origin ?
ASDs	=	Pediatric/Infant and Toddler Brain	+	Multiple Toxins	Origin ?
Regressive ASDs	=	Pediatric/Infant Toddler/Youth/Adult and Elderly Brain	+	Multiple Toxins and Medical Practice Errors	Origin ?

Brain Cell Mutations from Toxic Injuries: AUTISM, ASDs and ALZ © 2014 Dalva E. Yarrington

Scientific Title: *Vaccines, Toxins, Sensory Dysfunction and Regressive ASDs in the U. S.*

Keywords and Phrases:
Toxicity, etiology, Autism,
Regressive ASDs, vaccines,
pediatric toxins, longitudinal,
Cohort 80524, pediatric diagnostic failures, adverse reactions, stacked vaccines,
vaccine protocol, public health errors, epidemic, United States, library science,
data science, brain rewire, brain cell mutation, sensory dysfunction,
gastrointestinal disorders,
sickled intestinal cells, obesity,
ethyl-mercury, mercury poisoning,
prison pipeline under-diagnosis,
youth violence, policing and youth,
educational testing, error mitigation,
young adult suicide, maternal mortality rates, women and cardiovascular death
rate, parenting, abandonment, systemic failures, public health negligence,
congressional immunity, life quality, 1994, 2000, D. E. Yarrington,
Colorado, Minnesota, Texas, Mississippi, County Health Department, County
Government.
WHO Primary Registry and Trial Identifying Number
U1111-1165-4557

About the Program Developer and Researcher

D. E. Yarrington acquired her collegiate education at the University of Michigan from the School of Information and Library Science in the highly ranked and lauded academic division of Literature Science and Arts. Her special approach to her studies in ILS was under the approval of Dean Warner, former Director of the National Archives and Records Administration. Her library reference, law and government documents skills were honed under the instruction of esteemed scholars Thom Slavens and Joan Dorrance.

Her first evidence-based academic research was done at the Institute for Social Research on a well-funded Youth Policy Study under the leadership of a former Carter Administration, U.S. Justice Department appointee. From ISR she worked in academic computing "use policy" in the University of Michigan's Information Technology Division for the Office of the Vice Provost.

Following these academic achievements she spent two years serving during the Clinton administration on public health national service projects in Colorado and Minnesota. Her service leadership brought her to Washington D. C., and other leadership venues.

After positioning herself and her career to head a national non-profit, her son was brought to health-care calamity. This not only impacted her and her son, but also her collegiate and high school daughters.

At points during the past two decades she was able to take back her career from the demands of a health care calamity. In 2001 she planned, designed and established the Health Sciences Library at Jackson State University as the institution established a new school of Allied Health Sciences and a Program in Public Health. During her time at JSU she was able to deliver informatics and research training to hundreds of students and underpin JSU's health science funding accomplishments as a knowledge base specialist and resource SME.

Over the course of her career she created and or reorganized two policy library collections and one fully functional health sciences library facility and collection. Her work at JSU was visited by the sitting director of the NIH in 2003 and by other national public health professionals and lawmakers. Many more attended conference sessions and presentations lead by Ms. Yarrington on topics related to health science informatics, health disparities and collaboration. It is ground-work established between Ms. Yarrington and Ms. Ada Seltzer, the esteemed former director of the Ole' Miss Rowland Medical Library which now underpins many current JSU and Ole' Miss collaborations.

*"The work and career of this researcher has produced many long-standing achievements including The ASD Equation, TOUR MY ROOTS, The HR Blue Book and this program model (**What Can a County Do?**) is likely another. "*

ISBN: 978 -1070774015 $14.99

www.ingramcontent.com/pod-product-compliance
Lightning Source LLC
Chambersburg PA
CBHW070335290526
45791CB00003B/1340

* 9 7 8 1 0 7 0 7 7 4 0 1 5 *